Old Age
Is Always
15 Years Older
Than I Am

Old Age
Is Always
15 Years Older
Than I Am

Randy Voorhees

Andrews McMeel
Publishing®

a division of Andrews McMeel Universal

Andrews McMeel Publishing
a division of Andrews McMeel Universal
1130 Walnut Street, Kansas City, Missouri 64106

www.andrewsmcmeel.com

15 16 17 18 19 WKT 17 16 15 14 13

ISBN: 978-0-7407-1892-2

Library of Congress Catalog Card Number: 2001086774

Book design by Holly Ogden

─────── Attention: Schools and Businesses ───────

Andrews McMeel books are available at quantity discounts with bulk
purchase for educational, business, or sales promotional use. For
information, please e-mail the Andrews McMeel Publishing Special Sales
Department: specialsales@amuniversal.com.

This book is dedicated to
Ruth Winters, my "Nanny Ruth."
No one with her energy, spirit,
and love can ever be old.

■

Introduction

I chose old age as a subject because there doesn't seem to be any consensus on exactly what "old" is, and that fascinates me. We all have our own definition, and it often changes according to the context—a term of endearment for a spouse of many years, a pejorative describing the driver of the slow-moving car in front of us.

In my *Webster's Desk Dictionary* the word *old* is defined as "far advanced in years or life." I think that definition could be made better by adding five words at the end: "but not necessarily in both."

What I mean is that you can be old in years but young in life, or old in life but young in years. When I was twenty-five I was young in years, but, man, my body was well lived in. I was already old in life. My father is sixty-three, an age believed by many to be old, but he's just now enjoying retirement after forty-plus years of supporting a family, so he's young in life, and anxious to catch up.

I'm forty-two now, not an age that most people regard as old. If I were to die tomorrow people would say that I had "died young." I don't think so. My life has been spectacularly full, and though I hope to live another forty years, I'm already old in life. The bottom line is that everyone has a choice as to how to define what "old" is. No one can label you without your permission.

I'm sure that many of the quotations in this book will have you nodding, and just as many will have you shaking your head in disagreement. What I really hope is that you'll find something that will give you pause. And maybe, just maybe, something will make you change your own definition of "old." My favorite is by John Wayne, uttered before

Congress when the actor was asked to testify about aging in America. The Duke said, "Which of you is going to step up and put me out to pasture?"

I think Mr. Wayne speaks for most of us.

Randy Voorhees

Princeton, New Jersey

To me, old age is always fifteen years older than I am.

—Bernard Baruch, U.S. business executive

Old elephants limp off
to the hills to die;
old Americans go out to
the highway and drive
themselves to death
with huge cars.

—Hunter S. Thompson, U.S. author

I think all this talk about age
is foolish. Every time I'm
one year older, everyone else
is too.

—Gloria Swanson, U.S. actress

■

The excitement of learning
separates youth from old age.
As long as you are learning
you're not old.

—Rosalyn Sussman Yalow, U.S. medical physicist

If wrinkles must be written upon our brows, let them not be written upon the heart. The spirit should never grow old.

—James A. Garfield, U.S. president

Old age is not a disease;
it is a strength and
survivorship, triumph over
all kinds of vicissitudes
and disappointments,
trials and illnesses.

—Maggie Kuhn, U.S. activist and social worker

Old age is like everything else.
To make a success of it,
you've got to start young.

—Fred Astaire, U.S. dancer and actor

■

Outwardly I am eighty-three,
but inwardly I am every age,
with the emotions and
experience of each period.

—Elizabeth Coatsworth, U.S poet and children's author

Old age is like climbing
a mountain. You climb
from ledge to ledge.
The higher you get,
the more tired and
breathless you become,
but your views become
more extensive.

—Ingrid Bergman, Swedish actress

Old age is no place for sissies.

—Bette Davis, U.S. actress

Age is a question of mind
over matter. If you don't mind,
it doesn't matter.

—Satchel Paige, U.S. baseball player

■

Life would be infinitely happier
if we could only be born at the
age of eighty and gradually
approach eighteen.

—Mark Twain, U.S. writer and humorist

By the time we've made it,
we've had it.

—Malcolm Forbes, U.S. publisher

■

You can't help getting older,
but you don't have to get old.

—George Burns, U.S. comedian and actor

Just remember,
once you've over
the hill, you begin
to pick up speed.

—Charles Schulz, U.S. cartoonist

It's a mere moment in
a man's life between an
All-Star game and an
old-timer's game.

—Vin Scully, U.S. sportscaster

"Don't worry about senility,"
my grandfather used to say.
"When it hits you, you
won't know it."

—Bill Cosby, U.S. comedian, actor, and author

■

The man who views the world
at fifty the same as he did at
twenty has wasted thirty years
of his life.

—Muhammad Ali, U.S. heavyweight boxer

You're not too old until it takes longer to rest up than it does to get tired.

—Phog Allen, U.S. college basketball coach

When I was forty, my doctor advised me that a man in his forties shouldn't play tennis. I heeded his advice carefully and could hardly wait until I reached fifty to start again.

—Hugo Black, U.S. Supreme Court justice

Perhaps one has to be
very old before one learns
how to be amused
rather than shocked.

—Pearl S. Buck, U.S. author

When somebody says to me—
which they do like every five
years—"How does it feel to
be over the hill," my response is,
"I'm just heading up
the mountain."

—Joan Baez, U.S. singer

■

A man is not old until regrets
take the place of dreams.

—John Barrymore, U.S. actor

I have an understandable reluctance to pay much attention to the passage of time, and a certain animosity toward those who assume that if one is in his seventies he must have been a high school buddy of Abraham Lincoln.

—Fred De Cordova, U.S. television producer

Which of you is going to step up and put me out to pasture?

—John Wayne, U.S. actor

Men are like wine.
Some turn
to vinegar, but
the best improve
with age.

—Pope John XXIII

Wrinkles should
merely indicate
where smiles have been.

—Mark Twain, U.S. writer and humorist

■

Those [golf] clubs don't know
how old you are.

—Claudia Trevino, wife of
U.S. professional golfer Lee Trevino

Within I do not find
wrinkles and used heart,
but unspent youth.

—Ralph Waldo Emerson, U.S. poet, essayist, and lecturer

■

The trick is to grow up
without growing old.

—Frank Lloyd Wright, U.S. architect

Do not go gentle into
that good night,
Old age should burn
and rage at close of day;
Rage, rage against the
dying of the light.

—Dylan Thomas, Welsh poet

One should never
make one's debut
with a scandal;
one should reserve
that to give interest
to one's old age.

—Oscar Wilde, Irish wit, poet, and dramatist

God gave us memories
so that we might have roses
in December.

—James M. Barrie, Scottish novelist and dramatist

■

You know you're
getting old when the candles
cost more than the cake.

—Bob Hope, U.S. comedian and actor

When I was young
there was no respect
for the young, and now
that I'm old there is
no respect for the old.
I missed coming
and going.

—J. B. Priestley, English novelist,
playwright, and essayist

I've always thought that the stereotype of the dirty old man is really the creation of a dirty young man who wants the field to himself.

—Hugh Downs, U.S. television host

Old age isn't so bad
when you consider
the alternative.

—Maurice Chevalier, French actor and singer

■

Like a lot of the
fellows out here, I have a
furniture problem. My chest
has fallen into my drawers.

—Billy Casper, senior professional golfer

One of the delights
known to age,
and beyond the
grasp of youth,
is that of
Not Going.

—J. B. Priestley, English novelist, playwright, and essayist

There are three
periods
in life: youth,
middle age, and
"how well you
look."

—Nelson A. Rockefeller, U.S. vice president
and governor of New York

Competitiveness is a personality thing and competitive people don't become pushovers the day they turn fifty.

—Hale Irwin, senior professional golfer

A diplomat is a man
who always remembers
his wife's birthday but never
remembers her age.

—Robert Frost, U.S. poet

■

After thirty, a body has
a mind of its own.

—Bette Midler, U.S. actress and singer

Fun is like insurance; the older you get, the more it costs.

—Elbert Hubbard, U.S. editor, publisher, and author

A woman is
as old as she looks
before breakfast.

—Edgar Watson Howe, U.S. editor, novelist, and essayist

Nothing is more
responsible for the
good old days
than a bad memory.

—Robert Benchley, U.S. humorist, critic, and actor

A man is as old
as the woman he feels.

—Groucho Marx, U.S. comedian and actor

■

The young man who
has not wept is a savage,
and the old man who will
not laugh is a fool.

—George Santayana, Spanish-American
philosopher and poet

I have everything
now that I had
twenty years ago,
except now it's
all lower.

—Gypsy Rose Lee, U.S. exotic dancer

Inside every seventy-year-old is a thirty-five-year-old asking, "What happened?"

—Ann Landers, U.S. advice columnist

Age only matters
when one is aging.
Now that I have
arrived at a great age,
I might just as well
be twenty.

—Pablo Picasso, Spanish artist

To get back my youth
I would do anything in the
world, except take exercise,
get up early, or be respectable.

—Oscar Wilde, Irish wit, poet, and dramatist

■

I never think of the future.
It comes soon enough.

—Albert Einstein, German-born U.S. physicist

There is only one
thing wrong with
the younger generation—
a lot of us don't
belong to it anymore.

—Bernard Baruch, U.S. business executive

Middle age is when
you're sitting at home
on Saturday night and
the telephone rings and
you hope it isn't for you.

—Ogden Nash, U.S. poet and humorist

Time and tide
wait for no man,
but time always
stands still for a
woman of thirty.

—Robert Frost, U.S. poet

Years ago, we discovered
the exact point, the dead
center of middle age.
It occurs when you are
too young to take up golf
and too old to rush up
to the net.

—Franklin Pierce Adams, U.S. newspaper
columnist and humorist

Middle age is when
a man is always thinking that in
a week or two he will feel as
good as ever.

—Don Marquis, U.S. journalist and poet

■

In love, as in other matters,
the young are just beginners.

—Isaac Bashevis Singer, Polish-born
American novelist and essayist

The dead might as well try to speak to the living as the old to the young.

—Willa Cather, U.S. novelist

Nobody grows old by merely living a number of years. People grow old only by deserting their ideals. Years may wrinkle the skin, but to give up interest wrinkles the soul.

—Douglas MacArthur, U.S. army general

Middle age is when you've met so many people that every new person you meet reminds you of someone else.

—Ogden Nash, U.S. poet and humorist

■

I am long on ideas, but short on time. I expect to live to be only about a hundred.

—Thomas A. Edison, U.S. inventor

You know you're
getting old when all
the names in your
black book have
M.D. after them.

—Arnold Palmer, U.S. professional golfer

Age doesn't matter, unless you're a cheese.

—John Paul Getty, U.S. oil magnate

That's the trouble with us. We number everything. Take women, for example. I think they deserve to have more than twelve years between the ages of twenty-eight and forty.

—James Thurber, U.S. writer and cartoonist

Once you get past the fear of being responsible, it feels good. At forty, it suddenly seems unattractive to be a boy and very attractive to be a man.

—Paul Simon, U.S. singer and songwriter

This middle-life thing has become a phobia; people think it's got to be a big problem, when it's simply not. I know from real life that middle-aged people are very attractive. I feel I'm beating out all those guys who stay on rigid diets. They run; they go crazy; their skin is always in fabulous shape. I feel like I'm going to scoop the pot going the other way.

—Jack Nicholson, U.S. actor

Take it easy, that's all
you have to do.
Don't fight it.
You're the only one
who is passionately
interested in your age;
other people have
their own troubles.

—Dorothy Parker, U.S. writer, poet, and wit

I am not young enough
to know everything.

—Oscar Wilde, Irish wit, poet, and dramatist

■

The longer I live the more
I see that I am never wrong
about anything, and that all
the pains I have so humbly
taken to verify my notions
have only wasted my time.

—George Bernard Shaw, Irish-born dramatist and critic

The day of your thirtieth birthday you're going to wake up so relieved you'll think you've just won the lottery. Now you can get on with the next fifty or sixty years of your life and never worry about turning thirty again. The best part is: you're going to see how much better life is now that you're old enough to know better but still young enough to do it anyway.

—Julie Tilsner, U.S. writer

Almost all enduring
success comes to people
after they are forty.
For seldom does mature
judgment arrive
before then.

—Henry Ford, U.S. automobile magnate

I don't worry about
getting old. I'm old already.
Only young people worry
about getting old.

—George Burns, U.S. comedian and actor

■

Old age is the only disease
you don't look forward
to being cured of.

—From the movie *Citizen Kane*, 1941

A man's character never
changes radically
from youth to old age.
What happens is that
circumstances bring out
characteristics which
have not been obvious
to the superficial observer.

—Hesketh Pearson, English actor,
director, and biographer

Cherish all your happy
moments; they make a fine
cushion for old age.

—Booth Tarkington, U.S. novelist and dramatist

■

Getting older is like riding
a bicycle, if you don't
keep peddling, you'll fall.

—Claude Pepper, U.S. congressman

By the time we hit fifty,
we have learned our
hardest lessons. We have
found out that only a few
things are real important.
We have learned to
take life seriously,
but never ourselves.

—Marie Dressler, Canadian-born U.S. actress

Growing old is no more than
a bad habit which a busy man
has no time to form.

—André Maurois, French biographer,
novelist, and essayist

■

Middle age is when your
old classmates are so gray
and wrinkled and bald
they don't recognize you.

—Bennett Cerf, U.S. publisher and journalist

Musicians don't retire; they stop when there's no more music in them.

—Louis Armstrong, U.S. musician

We have no permanent
brains until we are forty.
Then they begin to harden,
presently they petrify,
then business begins.
Since forty I have been
regular about going to bed
and getting up—and that
is one of the main things.

—Mark Twain, U.S. writer and humorist

Retirement at sixty-five
is ridiculous. When I was
sixty-five I still had pimples.

—George Burns, U.S. comedian and actor

■

By common consent gray hairs
are a crown of glory; the only
object of respect that can
never excite envy.

—George Bancroft, U.S. historian

Gray hair is God's graffiti.

—Bill Cosby, U.S. comedian, actor, and author

In old age . . . we are like
a batch of letters.
We are no longer in the past,
we have arrived.

—Knut Hamsun, Norwegian novelist

■

In my youth I stressed freedom,
and in my old age I stress order.
I have made the great discovery
that liberty is a product of order.

—Will Durant, U.S. historian

Old age is the
most unexpected of all
the things that happen
to a man.

—Leon Trotsky, Russian revolutionary

■

My health is good;
it's my age that's bad.

—Roy Acuff, U.S. country music singer and songwriter

An archaeologist is the best
husband any woman can have;
the older she gets, the more
interested he is in her.

—Agatha Christie, English writer

■

The "good old times":
all times, when old, are good.

—Lord Byron, English poet

Be forever a student.
He and he alone is an
old man who feels that he
has learnt enough and
has no need for more
knowledge.

—Sivananda, Indian physician and sage

I am as old as my tongue
and older than my teeth.

—Jonathan Swift, Irish clergyman and satirist

■

A "Grand Old Man."
That means on our continent
anyone with snow white hair
who has kept out of jail
until eighty.

—Stephen Leacock, Canadian economist and humorist

Ain't nobody going to censor me, no, sir! I'm a hundred and one years old, and at my age, honey, I can say what I want!

—Annie Elizabeth Delany, U.S. dentist

■

An old young man will be a young old man.

—Benjamin Franklin, U.S. statesman, inventor, and writer

Every stage of human life,
except the last, is marked
out by certain and defined
limits; old age alone
has no precise and
determinate boundary.

—Marcus Tullius Cicero, Roman statesman and scholar

Experience is a great
advantage. The problem
is that when you get
the experience you're
too damned old to
do anything about it.

—Jimmy Connors, U.S. professional tennis player

Greatness is the dream of youth
realized in old age.

—Alfred-Victor de Vigny, French man of letters

■

Growing old's like being
increasingly penalized
for a crime
you haven't committed.

—Anthony Powell, English novelist

I have found it to
be true that the
older I've become
the better my life
has become.

—Rush Limbaugh, U.S. radio commentator and author

I was born old and
get younger every day.
At present I am
sixty years young.

—Herbert Beerbohm Tree, English actor

■

I will never give in to
old age until I become old.
And I'm not old yet!

—Tina Turner, U.S. singer

In youth one has tears
without grief, in old age
grief without tears.

—Jean Paul, German novelist

■

No one is so old as to think
he cannot live one more year.

—Marcus Tullius Cicero, Roman statesman and scholar

Old age is like
a plane flying
through a storm.
Once you're aboard
there's nothing
you can do.

—Golda Meir, Israeli political leader

I'll keep going until
my face falls off.

—Barbara Cartland, English novelist

■

Probably the happiest period
in life most frequently is
in middle age, when the eager
passions of youth are cooled,
and the infirmities of age
not yet begun.

—Thomas Arnold, English educator

Since it is the Other within us who is old, it is natural that the revelation of our age should come to us from outside—from others. We do not accept it willingly.

—Simone de Beauvoir, French writer

The belief that youth is the happiest time of life is founded on a fallacy. The happiest person is the person who thinks the most interesting thoughts, and we grow happier as we grow older.

—William Lyon Phelps, U.S. educator and journalist

The denunciation
of the young is a
necessary part of the
hygiene of older people,
and greatly assists
the circulation
of their blood.

—Logan Pearsall Smith, U.S.-English essayist and editor

The pleasure of one's effect
on other people still exists in
age—what's called making
a hit. But the hit is much rarer
and made of different stuff.

—Enid Bagnold, English novelist and playwright

■

The secret of genius is to
carry the spirit of the child
into old age, which means
never losing your enthusiasm.

—Aldous Huxley, English novelist and critic

The secret of
staying young is
to live honestly,
eat slowly, and
lie about your age.

—Lucille Ball, U.S. actress

When I was young,
I was told,
"You'll see,
when you're fifty."
I am fifty and I
haven't seen
a thing.

—Erik Satie, French composer

You end up as
you deserve. In old age
you must put up with
the face, the friends,
the health, and the children
you have earned.

—Fay Weldon, English novelist

Youth is the time of getting,
middle age of improving,
and old age of spending.

—Anne Bradstreet, U.S. poet

∎

You can be young without
money but you can't be old
without it.

—Tennessee Williams, U.S. playwright

It's daring and challenging
to be young and poor,
but never to be old
and poor. Whatever
resources of good health,
character, and fortitude
you bring to retirement,
remember, also,
to bring money.

—Jane Bryant Quinn, U.S. financial writer

In youth money is a convenience, an aid to pleasure. In age it is an absolute necessity, for when we are old we have to buy even consideration and politeness from those about us.

—Dorothy Dix, U.S. writer

The three
immutable facts:
You own stuff.
You will die.
Someone will
get that stuff.

—Jane Bryant Quinn, U.S. financial writer

There is no cure for birth
and death save to enjoy
the interval.

—George Santayana, Spanish-American
philosopher and poet

■

Life is better than death,
I believe, if only because it
is less boring, and because it
has fresh peaches in it.

—Alice Walker, U.S. novelist and poet

Women whose
identity depends more
on their outsides
than their insides
are dangerous when they
begin to age.

—Gloria Steinem, U.S. feminist

One should never trust a woman who tells one her real age. A woman who would tell that would tell anything.

—Oscar Wilde, Irish wit, poet, and dramatist

My experience is that
as soon as people are
old enough to know better,
they don't know anything
at all.

—Oscar Wilde, Irish wit, poet, and dramatist

■

Time himself is bald.

—William Shakespeare, English playwright,
poet, and actor

After a man is fifty
you can fool him by saying
he is smart, but you
can't fool him by saying
he is pretty.

—Edgar Watson Howe, U.S. editor, novelist, and essayist

If you pull out
a gray hair
seven will come
to its funeral.

—Pennsylvania German proverb

We do not count a man's years
until he has nothing else
to count.

—Ralph Waldo Emerson, U.S. poet, essayist, and lecturer

■

I love everything that's old—
old friends, old times,
old manners, old books,
old wine.

—Oliver Goldsmith, English essayist, poet, and novelist

Rest is
for the dead.

—Thomas Carlyle, Scottish historian and essayist

■

Old age is the
verdict of life.

—Amelia Barr, U.S. novelist and journalist

The love of retirement has, in all ages, adhered closely to those minds which have been most enlarged by knowledge, or elevated by genius.

—Samuel Johnson, English poet, essayist, and critic

To be seventy years old is like climbing the Alps. You reach a snow-covered summit, and see behind you the deep valley stretching miles and miles away, and before you other summits higher and whiter, which you may have strength to climb, or may not. Then you sit down and meditate and wonder which it will be.

—Henry Wadsworth Longfellow, U.S. poet

The young man
knows the rules,
but the old man
knows the exceptions.

—Oliver Wendell Holmes, Sr., U.S. writer

■

Adults are
obsolete children.

—Dr. Seuss (Theodor Seuss Geisel),
U.S writer and illustrator of children's books

After a certain number of years,
our faces become our
biographies.

—Cynthia Ozick, U.S. novelist and essayist

■

Age does not protect you
from love. But love,
to some extent,
protects you from age.

—Jeanne Moreau, French actor and director

When I no longer
thrill to the first snow
of the season,
I'll know I'm
growing old.

—Lady Bird Johnson, U.S. first lady

I don't know what the big deal
is about old age. Old people who
shine from inside look ten
to twenty years younger.

—Dolly Parton, U.S. country singer, songwriter, and actress

■

When grace is joined with
wrinkles, it is adorable.
There is an unspeakable dawn
in happy old age.

—Victor Hugo, French novelist, poet, and playwright

To age with dignity and with courage cuts close to what it is to be a man.

—Roger Kahn, U.S. writer

■

Growing older is not upsetting; being perceived as old is.

—Kenny Rogers, U.S. country singer, songwriter, and actor

If you carry
your childhood
with you, you
never grow older.

—Abraham Sutzkever, Russian Yiddish-language poet

The older you get,
the greater you were.

—Lee Grosscup, U.S. sportscaster

■

I have often thought what
a melancholy world this would
be without children—and
what an inhuman world,
without the aged.

—Samuel Taylor Coleridge, English poet,
critic, and philosopher

A young boy is a theory; an old man is a fact.

—Edgar Watson Howe, U.S. editor,
novelist, and essayist

You don't get to choose
how you're going to die.
Or when. You can only
decide how you're going
to live. Now.

—Joan Baez, U.S. singer

■

If you wait, all that happens
is that you get older.

—Larry McMurtry, U.S. novelist

Half our life is
spent trying to find
something to do
with the time we
have rushed
through life trying
to save.

—Will Rogers, U.S. humorist

Butterflies count
not months
but moments,
and yet have
time enough.

—Rabindranath Tagore, Bengali poet and mystic

You must have been warned against letting the golden hours slip by; but some of them are golden only because we let them slip by.

—James M. Barrie, Scottish dramatist and novelist

■

I knew a man who gave up smoking, drinking, sex, and food. He was healthy right up to the time he killed himself.

—Johnny Carson, U.S. television host

Things do not change,
we do.

—Henry David Thoreau, U.S. essayist, naturalist, and poet

■

Middle age is when
your age starts to show
around your middle.

—Bob Hope, U.S. comedian and actor

Time is
the thief you
cannot banish.

—Phyllis McGinley, U.S. poet and author

My parents didn't want to move to Florida, but they turned sixty, and it was the law.

—Jerry Seinfeld, U.S. comedian and actor

He decided to live forever,
or die in the attempt.

—Joseph Heller, U.S. novelist

■

Time does not become sacred
to us until we have lived it.

—John Burroughs, U.S. writer and naturalist

My eyes have seen much, but they are not weary. My ears have heard much, but they thirst for more.

—Rabindranath Tagore, Bengali poet and mystic

I am ready to meet
my Maker. Whether my
Maker is prepared for
the ordeal of meeting me
is another matter.

—Winston Churchill, English prime minister

I have my eighty-seventh birthday coming up and people ask what I'd more appreciate getting. I'll tell you: a paternity suit.

—George Burns, U.S. comedian and actor

■

I was born in 1962. True. And the room next to me was 1963.

—Joan Rivers, U.S. comedian and television host

Sex after ninety
is like trying to
shoot pool with
a rope.

—George Burns, U.S. comedian and actor

There are five essentials for a happy old age, and I enjoy them all: good health, sufficient money, friendship (including family), congenial surroundings, and continued activity. I put the last first.

—Nigel Nicolson, English writer

If youth but knew;
if age but could.

—Henri Estienne II, French printer

■

To see a young couple loving
each other is no wonder;
but to see an old couple loving
each other is the best
sight of all.

—William Makepeace Thackeray, English novelist

From thirty-five to forty-five women are old, and at forty-five the devil takes over, and they're beautiful, splendid, maternal, proud. The acidities are gone, and in their place reigns calm. They are worth going out to find, and because of them some men never grow old. When I see them my mouth waters.

—Jean-Baptiste Troigros, French restaurateur

All the best sands of my life are somehow getting into the wrong end of the hourglass. If I could only reverse it! Were it in my power to do so, would I?

—Thomas B. Aldrich, U.S. poet, writer, and editor

You know, when I first went into the movies Lionel Barrymore played my grandfather. Later he played my father and finally he played my husband. If he had lived, I'm sure I would have played his mother. That's the way it is in Hollywood. The men get younger and the women get older.

—Lillian Gish, U.S. actress

Every man's memory is
his private literature.

—Aldous Huxley, English novelist and critic

■

Measurement of life should be
proportioned rather to the
intensity of the experience
than to its actual length.

—Thomas Hardy, English poet and novelist

I won't be old
till my feet hurt,
and they only hurt when
I don't let 'em dance
enough, so I'll keep right
on dancing.

—Bill "Bojangles" Robinson, U.S. dancer

Paradoxical as it may seem,
to believe in youth
is to look backward;
to look forward we must
believe in age.

—Dorothy Sayers, English novelist

Young people can seldom understand that at seventy-six one is very much the same person one was at twenty-five, just as the chairman finds no difficulty at all in identifying with the junior clerk he once was, while his colleagues cannot imagine him anything but chairman.

—Nigel Nicolson, English writer

No matter how long he lives,
no man ever becomes as wise
as the average woman of
forty-eight.

—H. L. Mencken, U.S. writer and humorist

■

The best years are the forties:
after fifty a man begins to
deteriorate. But in the forties
he is at maximum of his villainy.

—H. L. Mencken, U.S. writer and humorist

I wouldn't go back in time for anything in the world. When I was younger, I was defenseless . . . fearful that I couldn't live up to other people's standards. Now I'm stronger, able to take care of myself, enjoying my work and my time on this planet.

—Ellen Burstyn, U.S. actress

When I was
twenty-seven,
I felt like a pebble
on the beach.
Now I feel like
the whole beach.

—Shirley MacLaine, U.S. actress

It's nothing that really worries me. If it was just down to me, I think I would hardly notice it. Plus, with the kids, I don't particularly want to be youthful. I want to be a father. Being youthful, rock-'n'-roll, I've done that for so long. I'm ready to move over a bit to maturity.

—Paul McCartney, English singer and songwriter

No matter how often I
tell people I'm thirty-nine
some of them refuse to
believe I'm that old.

—Jack Benny, U.S. radio and television personality

■

I believe every woman,
especially those over forty,
needs the rejuvenation that
a few moments alone
can provide.

—Sophia Loren, Italian actress

I won't be able to do what I'm doing forever. There aren't that many scripts floating around for fifty-year-old chicks.

—Cher, U.S. singer and actress

When I look around me, I'm beginning to think a lot of guys I see nowadays are forty before they develop a great deal of emotional maturity. I think we men mature a little later in life.

—Ted Danson, U.S. actor

I eat all the time—
anything and everything,
in unbelievable amounts.
It's funny—I was always
very disciplined through
my twenties and thirties,
and now . . . I'm ready to
party when everybody's
decided to become
disciplined.

—Farrah Fawcett, U.S. actress

Crossing the street in
New York keeps old people
young—if they make it.

—Andy Rooney, U.S. writer and humorist

∎

Jewelry takes people's
minds off your wrinkles.

—Sonja Henie, Norwegian figure skater

I'm here to say that we will get the jobs we want when we are past forty, and that we will have sex until we die. Life doesn't end when your flip blond hairdo is cut off.

—Sally Jessy Raphael, U.S. television host

Grow up, and that is a
terribly hard thing to do.
It is much easier to skip it
and go from one childhood
to another.

—F. Scott Fitzgerald, U.S. writer

■

An old man in a house
is a good sign.

—Benjamin Franklin, U.S. statesman, inventor, and writer

In all of the theories about why so many people have attacks of wackiness when they reach middle age—resign from the bank to go live in a van with a teen-age mushroom gatherer, and that sort of thing—one factor has been neglected: When someone reaches middle age, people he knows begin to get put in charge of things, and knowing what he knows about the people who are being put in charge of things scares the hell out of him.

—Calvin Trillin, U.S. writer

Mid-life crises in reality
are quite rare. The more typical
experience is a feeling of
contentment and satisfaction in
the middle years of life.

—Dr. Ronald Kessler, U.S. doctor

■

It's great getting old.

—Harrison Ford, U.S. actor

The French are true romantics. They feel the only difference between a man of forty and one of seventy is thirty years of experience.

—Maurice Chevalier, French actor and singer

■

Men reach their sexual peak at eighteen. Women reach theirs at forty-five. Do you get the feeling God is playing a practical joke?

—Rita Rudner, U.S. comedian, essayist, and actress

I know a lot of men who
are healthier at age fifty
than they have ever been
before, because a lot of
their fear is gone.

—Robert Bly, U.S. poet

Twenty can't be expected to tolerate sixty in all things, and sixty gets bored stiff with twenty's eternal love affairs.

—Emily Carr, Canadian artist and writer

But though an old man,
I am but a young gardener.

—Thomas Jefferson, U.S. president

■

Many people die at
twenty-five and aren't buried
until they are seventy-five.

—Benjamin Franklin, U.S. statesman, inventor, and writer

I was thirty-seven when I went to work writing the column. I was too old for a paper route, too young for Social Security, and too tired for an affair.

—Erma Bombeck, U.S. journalist, author, and humorist

■

All that I know I learned after I was thirty.

—Georges Clemenceau, French statesman

The boy gathers materials for a temple, and then when he is thirty, concludes to build a woodshed.

—Henry David Thoreau, U.S. essayist, naturalist, and poet

Wisdom and penetration
are the fruit of experience, not
the lessons of
retirement and leisure.

—Abigail Adams, U.S. first lady

■

In terms of my store of
emotional experience,
it now has many more aisles
than twenty years ago.

—Didi Conn, U.S. actress

I can't say I feel fifty, because the way my mother and grandmother looked when I was growing up is not happening anymore.

—Tina Turner, U.S. singer

Laugh, and you'll live
without Medicaid until
you're one hundred.

—Julie Newmar, U.S. actress

■

Women are just
beginning at forty.
At fifty you
hit your power.

—Lauren Hutton, U.S. supermodel

I think America is
realizing that there's
a beauty that comes with
knowledge and experience.
I feel more beautiful now
in many ways.

—Cheryl Tiegs, U.S. supermodel

I just don't think of age and time in respect of years. I just have too much experience of people in their seventies who are vigorous and useful and people who are thirty-five that are in lousy physical shape and can't think straight. I don't think age has that much to do with it.

—Harrison Ford, U.S. actor

You're only
young once,
but you can be
immature
all your life.

—Charles Scoggins

If you take all the experience and judgment of men over fifty out of the world, there wouldn't be enough left to run it.

—Henry Ford, U.S. automobile magnate

Most men who are not
married by the age of thirty-five
are either homosexual or
really smart.

—Becky Rodenbeck

■

The lovely thing about
being forty is that you can
appreciate twenty-five-year-old
men more.

—Colleen McCullough, Australian novelist

When the grandmothers of today hear the word "Chippendales," they don't necessarily think of chairs.

—Jean Kerr, U.S. humorist, author, and playwright

People ask how
I feel about
getting old. I tell
them I have the
same question.
I'm learning as I go.

—Paul Simon, U.S. singer and songwriter

We live in deeds, not years;
in thoughts, not figures
on a dial. We should count
time by heart throbs.
He most lives who thinks
most, feels the noblest,
acts the best.

—Philip James Bailey, English poet

Character contributes
to beauty. It fortifies a woman
as her youth fades.

—Jacqueline Bisset, English actress

■

I live in that solitude which
is painful in youth, but delicious
in the years of maturity.

—Albert Einstein, German-born U.S. physicist

Youth is the gift of nature, but age is a work of art.

—Garson Kanin, U.S. playwright and director

People have this obsession.
They want you to be
like you were in 1969.
They want you to,
because otherwise their
youth goes with you. . . .
It's very selfish, but
it's understandable.

—Mick Jagger, English singer and songwriter

I'd like to be a bigger and more knowledgeable person ten years from now than I am today. I think that, for all of us, as we grow older, we must discipline ourselves to continue expanding, broadening, learning, keeping our minds active and open.

—Clint Eastwood, U.S. actor and director

If you get to thirty-five
and your job still involves
wearing a name tag,
you've probably made a
serious vocational error.

—Dennis Miller, U.S. comedian and television personality

■

I may be an antique like
the [Rolling] Stones,
but antiques are valuable.

—Billy Joel, U.S. singer and songwriter

People do not retire.
They are retired by others.

—Duke Ellington, U.S. bandleader and composer

■

There's nothing worse
than being an
aging young person.

—Richard Pryor, U.S. comedian and actor

You know, by the time you reach my age, you've made plenty of mistakes if you've lived your life properly.

—Ronald Reagan, U.S. president

It's ill-becoming
for an old broad to
sing about how
bad she wants it.
But occasionally
we do.

—Lena Horne, U.S. singer and actress

There are only three ages for women in Hollywood— Babe, District Attorney, and Driving Miss Daisy.

—Goldie Hawn, U.S. actress

■

As you get older, the pickings get slimmer, but the people don't.

—Carrie Fisher, U.S. actress and author

I like who I am. Other people may not. I'm comfortable. I feel freer now. I don't want growing older to matter to me.

—Meryl Streep, U.S. actress

■

I was very sophisticated when I was seventeen. When I was fourteen, I was the oldest I ever was. . . . I've been getting younger ever since.

—Shirley Temple Black, U.S. actress and diplomat

The best age
is the age you are.

—Maggie Kuhn, U.S. activist and social worker

One does not get better
but different and older
and that is always a pleasure.

—Gertrude Stein, U.S. author

■

In the name of Hypocrites,
doctors have invented the most
exquisite form of torture ever
known to man: survival.

—Luis Buñuel, Spanish film director

I'm a little older now. I've moved from the sandwich generation to the club sandwich generation.

—Ellen Goodman, U.S. newspaper columnist

Learning and sex until rigor mortis.

—Maggie Kuhn, U.S. activist and social worker

Thirty was so strange for me. I've really had to come to terms with the fact that I am now a walking and talking adult.

—Matt Dillon, U.S. actor

It's no longer a question
of staying healthy. It's a question
of finding a sickness you like.

—Jackie Mason, U.S. comedian

■

Beauty comes in all ages,
colors, shapes, and forms.
God never makes junk.

—Kathy Ireland, U.S. model

It really costs me a lot emotionally to watch myself on-screen. I think of myself, and I feel like I'm quite young, and then I look at this old man with the baggy chins and the tired eyes and the receding hairline and all that.

—Gene Hackman, U.S. actor

Old age is an excellent time for outrage. My goal is to say or do at least one outrageous thing every week.

—Maggie Kuhn, U.S. activist and social worker

I begin to realize that I am growing old: The taxi driver calls me "Pop" instead of "Buddy."

—Alexander Woollcott, U.S. author, critic, and actor

■

I enjoy my wrinkles and regard them as badges of distinction—I've worked hard for them!

—Maggie Kuhn, U.S. activist and social worker

The aging process
has you firmly
in its grasp
if you never
get the urge to
throw a snowball.

—Doug Larson

When you're fifty you start thinking about things you haven't thought about before. I used to think getting old was about vanity, but actually it's about losing people you love. Getting wrinkles is trivial.

—Joyce Carol Oates, U.S. novelist and poet

Getting old is a
fascination thing.
The older you get, the older
you want to get.

—Keith Richards, English rock guitarist and songwriter

■

Middle age is when the
best exercise is one of discretion.

—Laurence J. Peter, Canadian-U.S. educator and author

From birth to age eighteen, a girl needs good parents. From eighteen to thirty-five, she needs good looks. From thirty-five to fifty-five, she needs a good personality. From fifty-five on, she needs good cash.

—Sophie Tucker, U.S. singer

I have long thought that the aging process could be slowed down if it had to work its way through Congress.

—George H. W. Bush, U.S. president

When I grow up,
I want to be a little boy.

—Joseph Heller, U.S. novelist

■

I've always believed
in the adage that the secret
of eternal youth is
arrested development.

—Alice Roosevelt Longworth, U.S. writer

I have no romantic feelings about age. Either you are interesting at any age or you are not. There is nothing particularly interesting about being old—or being young, for that matter.

—Katharine Hepburn, U.S. actress

The trouble with class reunions
is that old flames
have become even older.

—Doug Larson

■

The older you get,
the more important it is
not to act your age.

—Ashleigh Brilliant, British-born U.S. writer,
cartoonist, and columnist

The real sadness of fifty
is not that you change
so much but that you
change so little. . . .
My only birthday
resolution is to change
some of my habits
every year, even if
for the worse.

—Max Lerner, U.S. political columnist and educator

The great comfort
of turning
forty-nine is the
realization that
you are now too old
to die young.

—Paul Dickson, U.S. writer

How it rejoices a middle-aged
woman when her husband
criticizes a pretty girl!

—Mignon McLaughlin, U.S. aphorist

■

Middle age—by which I
mean anything over twenty
and under ninety.

—A. A. Milne, English writer

At fifty everyone has the face he deserves.

—George Orwell, English novelist, essayist, and critic

Middle age is
when anything new
in the way you feel
is most likely
a symptom.

—Laurence J. Peter, Canadian-U.S. educator and author

Middle age is when you're faced with two temptations and you choose the one that will get you home by nine o'clock.

—Ronald Reagan, U.S. president

■

I think of myself as I was twenty-five years ago. Then I look in a mirror and see an old bastard and I realize it's me.

—Dave Allen, Irish comedian

The older I grow,
the more I distrust
the familiar
doctrine that age
brings wisdom.

—H. L. Mencken, U.S. writer and critic

You all of a sudden realize
that you are being ruled
by people you went to high
school with. You all of a
sudden catch on that life is
nothing but high school . . .
class officers, cheerleaders,
and all.

—Kurt Vonnegut, U.S. novelist

Old age is a special problem for me because I've never been able to shed the mental image I have of myself—a lad of about nineteen.

—E. B. White, U.S. essayist, literary stylist, and writer

There are three classes of elderly women; first, that dear old soul; second, that old woman; third, that old witch.

—Samuel Taylor Coleridge, English poet, critic, and philosopher

■

When you win, you're an old pro. When you lose you're an old man.

—Charlie Conerly, U.S. professional football player

No man is ever old enough
to know better.

—Holbrook Jackson, English journalist,
editor, and author

■

Older women are best
because they always think
they may be doing it
for the last time.

—Ian Fleming, English writer

At sixty . . . the sexual preoccupation, when it hits you, seems somewhat sharper, as if it were an elderly malady, like gout.

—Edmund Wilson, U.S. critic and essayist

Discussing how old you are
is the temple of boredom.

—Ruth Gordon, U.S. actress

■

The older one grows
the more one
likes indecency.

—Virginia Woolf, English author

Put cotton in your ears
and pebbles in your shoes.
Pull on rubber gloves.
Smear Vasoline over
your glasses, and there
you have it:
instant old age.

—Malcolm Cowley, U.S. literary critic
and social historian

Sure, I'm for helping the elderly.
I'm going to be old someday.

—Lillian Carter, U.S. nurse and mother of
President Jimmy Carter

■

If you live long enough,
you're revered—
rather like an old building.

—Katharine Hepburn, U.S. actress

If God had to give
a woman wrinkles,
He might at least
have put them
on the soles
of her feet.

—Ninon de Lenclos, French society figure and courtesan

It has been said that there is no fool like an old fool, except a young fool. But the young fool has first to grow up to be an old fool to realize what a damn fool he was when he was a young fool.

—Harold Macmillan, English politician

One of the many pleasures
of old age is giving things up.

—Malcolm Muggeridge

■

Retirement must be wonderful.
I mean, you can suck in
your stomach for only so long.

—Burt Reynolds, U.S. actor

I'm saving that rocker for
the day when I feel as old
as I really am.

—Dwight Eisenhower, U.S. president

■

Most people say that
you get old, you have to
give things up. I think you get
old because you give things up.

—Theodore F. Green, U.S. senator

I think I'm the Picasso
of mime. At eighty, Picasso
was young. If I keep
my fitness, I have at least
another ten years. It's an
encouragement for all men
in their fifties, sixties,
and seventies. I don't think
of age. I think of life
and creation.

—Marcel Marceau, French mime

A mother never realizes
that her children are
no longer children.

—Holbrook Jackson, English journalist, editor, and author

■

When old people speak it is
not because of the sweetness
of words in our mouths;
it is because we see something
which you do not see.

—Chinua Achebe, Nigerian novelist

Allow me to put
the record straight.
I am forty-six and
have been for
some years past.

—Erica Jong, U.S. novelist

Keep breathing.

—Sophie Tucker, U.S. singer

You know you're old
when you've lost
all your marvels.

—Merry Browne

■

Do not worry about
avoiding temptation.
As you grow older
it will avoid you.

—Joey Adams, U.S. comedian and author

Men don't get smarter
when they grow older.
They just lose their hair.

—Claudette Colbert, French-born U.S. actress

■

They tell you that you'll lose
your mind when you grow older.
What they don't tell you is
that you won't miss it much.

—Malcolm Cowley, U.S. literary critic and social historian

Old minds are like old horses; you must exercise them if you wish to keep them in working order.

—John Quincy Adams, U.S. president

To know how to
grow old
is the master-work
of wisdom,
and one of the
most difficult chapters
in the great art
of living.

—Henri Frédéric Amiel, Swiss poet and philosopher

The older I get, the greater
power I seem to have to help
the world; I am like a
snowball—the farther I am
rolled the more I gain.

—Susan B. Anthony, U.S. social reformer and suffragist

■

The people who are always
hankering loudest for some
golden yesteryear usually
drive new cars.

—Russell Baker, U.S. journalist, author, and humorist

As I grow older, I pay less
attention to what men say.
I just watch what they do.

—Andrew Carnegie, U.S. industrialist and philanthropist

■

We all have our "good old days"
tucked away inside our hearts,
and we return to them
in daydreams like cats to
favorite armchairs.

—Brian Carter, U.S. biologist and writer

To be old is to be part
of a huge and ordinary
multitude. . . .
The reason why
old age was venerated
in the past was because
it was extraordinary.

—Ronald Blythe

I am an old scholar,
better-looking now
than when I was young.
That's what sitting
on your ass does
to your face.

—Leonard Cohen, Canadian singer and songwriter

The man who is too old
to learn was probably always
too old to learn.

—Henry S. Haskins

■

Never think any oldish thoughts.
It's oldish thoughts that
make a person old.

—James A. Farley, English physicist and chemist

Women are not forgiven for aging. Bob Redford's lines of distinction are my old-age wrinkles.

—Jane Fonda, U.S. actress

■

If a day goes by that don't change some of your old notions for new ones, that is just about like trying to milk a dead cow.

—Woody Guthrie, U.S. folksinger and songwriter

Too many people grow up. That's the real trouble with the world. . . . They don't remember what it's like to be twelve years old.

—Walt Disney, U.S. movie producer

My son is seven years old. I am fifty-four. It has taken me a great many years to reach that age. I am more respected in the community, I am stronger, I am more intelligent and I think I am better than he is. I don't want to be a pal, I want to be a father.

—Clifton Fadiman, U.S. radio performer and author

If you don't learn to laugh
at troubles, you won't have
anything to laugh at when
you're old.

—Edgar Watson Howe, U.S. editor, novelist, and essayist

■

I look forward to growing old
and wise and audacious.

—Glenda Jackson, British-born U.S. actress

Old age, believe me, is a good and pleasant thing. It is true you are gently shouldered off the stage, but then you are given such a comfortable front stall as spectator.

—Jane Harrison, English scholar, writer and archaeologist

I wouldn't have turned out the
way I was if I didn't have all
those old-fashioned values
to rebel against.

—Madonna, U.S. singer and actress

■

You don't have to be old in
America to say of a world you
lived in: That world is gone.

—Peggy Noonan, U.S. writer

Develop your eccentricities while you're young. That way, when you get old, people won't think you're going gaga.

—David Ogilvy, U.S. advertising executive

My greatest enemy is reality.
I have fought it successfully
for thirty years.

—Margaret Anderson, U.S. editor

■

Old people shouldn't eat
health foods. They need all the
preservatives they can get.

—Robert Orben, U.S. editor and writer

If in the last few years you haven't discarded a major opinion or acquired a new one, check your pulse. You may be dead.

—Gelett Burgess, U.S. writer, poet, humorist, and illlustrator

I mean, don't forget the earth's about five thousand million years old, at least. Who can afford to live in the past?

—Harold Pinter, English playwright

■

We need old friends to help us grow old and new friends to help us stay young.

—Letty Cottin Pogrebin, U.S. writer, editor, and columnist

Every man is enthusiastic at times. One man has enthusiasm for thirty minutes—another for thirty days, but it is the man who has it for thirty years who makes a success of his life.

—Edward B. Butler, Welsh actor

Sometimes I would almost rather have people take away years of my life than take away a moment.

—Pearl S. Buck, U.S. author

■

Change excites me. I am fifty years old. It's when the mind catches up with the body.

—Raquel Welch, U.S. actress and model

It is strange . . . that the years teach us patience; that the shorter our time, the greater our capacity for waiting.

—Elizabeth Taylor, British-born U.S. actress

There are years that ask
questions and years that answer.

—Zora Neale Hurston, U.S. dramatist and author

■

I was forced to live far beyond
my years when just a child,
now I have reversed the
order and I intend to
remain young indefinitely.

—Mary Pickford, Canadian-born U.S. actress

Wrinkles are hereditary. Parents get them from their children.

—Doris Day, U.S. singer and actress

■

Happiness is an imaginary condition formerly often attributed by the living to the dead, now usually attributed by adults to children, and by children to adults.

—Thomas Szasz, U.S. psychiatrist and educator

Boys are beyond the range of anybody's sure understanding, at least when they are between the ages of eighteen months and ninety years.

—James Thurber, U.S. writer and cartoonist

The only thing I regret about my past is the length of it. If I had to live my life again, I'd make the same mistakes, only sooner.

—Tallulah Bankhead, U.S. actress

What I look forward to
is continued immaturity
followed by death.

—Dave Barry, U.S. columnist, humorist, and author

■

True maturity is only reached
when a man realizes he has
become a father figure to his
girlfriends' boyfriends and
he accepts it.

—Larry McMurtry, U.S. novelist

To yackety-yak about the past is for me time lost. Every morning I wake up saying, "I'm still alive— a miracle." And so I keep on pushing.

—Jacques Cousteau, French explorer

Sooner or later we all discover that the important moments in life are not the advertised ones, not the birthdays, the graduations, the weddings, not the great goals achieved. The real milestones are less prepossessing. They come to the door of memory.

—Susan B. Anthony, U.S. social reformer and suffragist

Those who contemplate the beauty of the earth find reserves of strength that will endure as long as life lasts.

—Rachel Carson, U.S. biologist and writer

As you get older, you find
that often the wheat,
disentangling itself from the
chaff, comes out to meet you.

—Gwendolyn Brooks, U.S. poet

■

After you're older, two things
are possibly more important
than others: health and money.

—Helen Gurley Brown, U.S. editor and author

The invention of the teenager was a mistake. Once you identify a period of life in which people get to stay out late, but don't have to pay taxes—naturally, nobody wants to live any other way.

—Judith Martin, U.S. author and journalist

In later life, as in earlier,
only a few persons
influence the formation
of our character; the
multitude pass us by
like a distant army.

—Jean Paul, German novelist

If a thing is old,
it is a sign that it is fit to live.
The guarantee of continuity
is quality.

—Edward Rickenbacker, U.S. war hero
and airline executive

■

If you're old,
don't try to change yourself,
change your environment.

—B. F. Skinner, U.S. psychologist and author

Your sons weren't made like you. That's what grandchildren are for.

—Jane Smiley, U.S. novelist

There are only two things a child will share willingly—communicable diseases and his mother's age.

—Dr. Benjamin Spock, U.S. physician and author